page as bone – ink as blood

PAGE AS BONE – INK AS BLOOD

POEMS BY
JÓNÍNA KIRTON

Talonbooks

Talonbooks
9259 Shaughnessy Street, Vancouver, British Columbia, Canada V6P 6R4
www.talonbooks.com

Talonbooks is located on xʷməθkʷəy̓əm, Sḵwx̱wú7mesh, and səl̓ilwətaʔɬ Lands.

Second printing: 2019

Typeset in Dante
Printed and bound in Canada on 100% post-consumer recycled paper
Cover design by Typesmith

Talonbooks gratefully acknowledges the financial support of the Canada Council for the Arts, the Government of Canada through the Canada Book Fund, and the Province of British Columbia through the British Columbia Arts Council and the Book Publishing Tax Credit.

Library and Archives Canada Cataloguing in Publication

Kirton, Jónína, 1955–, author
     Page as bone – ink as blood : poems / Jónína Kirton.
ISBN 978-0-88922-923-5 (pbk.)

     I. Title.
PS8621.I785P33 2015   C811'.6   C2014-907068-3

The voices of the grandmothers and grandfathers compel me to speak of the worth of our people and the beauty that surrounds us, to banish the profaning of ourselves, and to ease pain. I carry the language of the voice of the land and the valiance of the people and I will not be silenced by tyranny.

— JEANNETTE ARMSTRONG

Contents

page as bone
ink as blood
drumbeat the call
smoke the signal

at night my dance card full
dress white lace   cape fringed   soft deerskin

      black patent leather shoes dipped in ink

trace letters   words   across the white linen floor
in my hair a peacock feather glistens

      the words emit a fragrance that at first I do not recognize

I lift my head, close my eyes, and in the arms

of the Creator   smell cedar

Half-Breed

Mother loved a white god.
Married an Indian.
Their only girl came first.

She dressed me in white lace   white booties
carefully placed me in a "proper" pram.
Yet the question persisted
where did you get her?

Later whitening cream
the warnings   *comb your hair!*
you look like a dirty little Indian!
And whispering between even us
where did you get her?

In school I learned
the word *squaw.*
Listened to Cher's "Half-Breed" over and over
tried to forget
where did you get her?

the doorbell

too soon in life I could see
what others could not see
at night a *dark potential* would reveal itself
in dreams before my brother's passing
        warnings of a watery death

missing   he came once more

rang the doorbell   only I heard

buoyant   on our doorstep   he dripped water

      let me know he was happy

not lost   was hiding

the next day they found him in the water

crone

If, while riding a horse overland, a man should come upon a
woman spinning, then that is a very bad sign; he should turn
around and take another way.

— JACOB GRIMM

i
every family has a historian
(from the distaff side of the family)
she is one-third storyteller
one-third publicist   one-third archivist
locked in the tower   her story will be another
version of the miller's daughter in *Rumpelstiltskin*
she must sit   spin   and with her distaff   spindle

turn straw truth into gold

ii
weaving begins with spinning
    in my loom's shuttle   the threads are not golden
my story captured in a web   a criss-crossing of my own making
       more wagon goddess than miller's daughter
my loom weighted with severed heads

     the shuttles stone arrows
crude warlike   my warp viscera
     I sing songs of carnage   make linen from flax

         protect unborn children

iii

now a crone   I wear my story   –   a seamless robe
which includes
            the authorized versions
what I think I know
            what I would like to know
threads I weave by day   unravel
                        by night

revelation

Grandma has left us
is she with the 144,000?

                                        was she anointed   faithful
                                            now a spirit creature?

                        – or –

in a state of non-existence

                        – or –

                                        a remnant   resurrected
                                            with the little flock
                                                the great crowd

                        – or –

                                                in heaven?

how hard she tried to convert her children
her funeral service a last pitch
filled with messages of how we could all be together again

            17   –   she had 17 children

their wives   their husbands   and their children

            equals (=) 79

this not counting second or third   husbands   wives
(there aren't many of those)
minus stepchildren   her brothers   sisters
how long would it take
to get to 144,000?

how many generations   resurrected
before we fill Jehovah's heaven

leaving no room for anyone else?

obsidian

at my centre   molten rock
rift zones   filled with lava

tectonically induced fractures

layered fault lines
unexpected shifts
leave viscous pathways
a certain blackness necessary for growth

thin

when I woke, you were gone
       in my dreams you were there, feel of you
as familiar to me as if it were yesterday that you

            last put your cheek

                        on my cheek

this thin veil of reality – altered in sleep –
allows access to those gone on   they beckon
hoping to remind us they are there
rest in peace (not to be assumed)
yet many times we say
    they are in a better place now (as if we know)
many have visited me
I can tell you, they have regrets
they do worry about those left behind

        – their message is always the same –
          they did not know
           how much they loved you

loved life on this side of the thin veil

dear pain

what is it that you want from me?
I try to work with you   hot baths
Epsom salts   stretches   walks
and when necessary, Percocet
but it is never enough   you always want more

without you I could do so much more
(at least that is what I tell myself)

you are my father's voice   –   the one that says I am a *slut*
tho' married   a mother   you still try that trick until ...

    I want
                        sex   no more

you take, and take my passion   ability to write   memory
        my desire   –   but each day I fight back
take pills   meditate   pray to dull your voice
    to lessen your control

just as he would in the night   you wake me up
    while others sleep   we "converse"
I try not to shout at you   –   occasionally you make me cry
        often you make me beg
you are so like him
his voice inside me   –   harsh as steel-toed boots
marching   sometimes kicking
cold   words   dark   nights leave me
sensitive to the light   I hide

hungry ghosts

you must not speak of the dead
their visits in the night
how they touch your forehead pass through you
      lie down beside you

every night they watch you sleep
wonder where you have gone
for the dead cannot dream

missing their bones
they live on in yours
your gait familiar to them
as theirs once was

always cold, they sit by the fire
occasionally the rocking chair moves
every night they look over your shoulder

      wish you read more poetry

immaterial

a man stands on a bridge
photographs the sunset
what he does not know
is that yesterday
a man stood there
only to fall over the edge
the dead weight
of his despair
dragged him to
the bottom and now
he looks up through
the murky water, asks

what colour is the sunset today?

unclaimed baggage

do you ever wonder if the skeletons in your closet chatter?
or simply rattle?   suspended on hangers
        no muscle to hold them up
skinless   they summon dignity
point their spiny fingers at one another
YOU belong here! I do not ...   as they compare stories
the great-great-grandmother whose only child
the offspring of a maid and a master
later disappeared in the small country of Iceland
          no trace of her ever found

going further back in those lands   the family curse

        a descendant killed by sorcery

documented by the town folk   this one   one to be afraid of
who knows how long those ill wishes last?
that skeleton browning   brittle
can barely lift its head   never argues with the others
and then there's the *one little, two little, three little Indians*

              shoved way into the back

they sing   powwow songs
hoping not to remember   how Father's sister knew

          the whole football team

missing

your secret keeps whispering in my ear
says that you're ignoring it   that you kicked it out
tired of eating out of garbage cans
thinks it deserves a place at the table
says it did nothing except
        whisper to you in the night

lucidity

the product of six celestial beings   the bride of Christ
she sits in the hallway   dons a blue sequined shower cap
over long dark hair   more model than patient
             resting elbow on bent knee
the other foot dangles   swings as she spreads love

             only here because "they" need her

but the yellow hospital pajamas give her away

pale from lack of sunlight, she argues, asks the nurses
would I not do better if I could go outside, feel the air?
her insistence rewarded with a locked door behind which
she sings at the top of her lungs until sufficiently medicated

             compliance sought at any cost

later at a review panel, tales are told of her adventures
scissors cut carpets   *there are dead people under there*
three hours later, tired   she offers everyone candy
and when asked if she has anything else to say
she invites the doctor to read her poem
reminds him that she speaks in metaphors

             a lyricist, in love with love

and I wonder might she be *the bride of Christ*
in her blue sequined shower cap
holding court in the dining hall   spreading love
until compliance leaves her dry mouthed,   dull

scry

thin fingers trace rivers on maps with dark edges
on the wall all mirrors painted black for scrying
in those surfaces she looks for him
the child that fell into the river
his body found   later embalmed   now in a grave
    just down the street
        but she wonders   *what of his soul?*

hoping for visitations, she readies herself every night
prays   as her fingers trace all rivers
on the maps in the room of her divining
once ready she gazes into the black mirrors by candlelight
hoping to catch a glimpse of his reflection

        but he is never there

she does not know   he is not in the dark
he is in the field by the river where he fell
he runs there every day   hoping to see her

        before he falls in again

collective history

divergent lives meet at the border
Bogart's on the edge, where the North End meets downtown
Winnipeg's Studio 54, an old bank building
where life's deserters cross over
meet on the dance floor
Tuxedo Park boys, rich   looking to drown out the voices of obligation
craved the drugs the arsonist and the boxer provided
Portage and Main, an intersection where need meets want
and amid the inner rubble, the marble pillars, we all play
a transactional game where everyone tries to trade up

in his tower the DJ – a demigod of nightly worship
takes us into trance dance
encoded in our bodies a collective history
of days when we hung mirrors on trees
where pain and pleasure reflected visceral truths

we are all crows   like shiny things
the mirror ball spinning light   offers flickering fractures
but never invites reflection

heavy with memory my body finds wordless ways
to stir cellular recall   my turtle mind slow steady
walks me to the dance floor
where my snake body dances me

I am in a moving sea of sound
within the beginning of time
an elemental dreaming   born of water
inside, the oracle divines my salvation
but I am still suspicious of my body's story
leave a trail of marooned memories   frozen fragments
parts of me are scattered on the altar of one-night stands

once home haunted by my losses, I weep   water meets wood
as I lie on the hardwood floor, contemplate
          the collective curse in our genes
a shame carrier   I am doomed to wander
      I am a vortex of empty space, where
my bitterness and brooding calls out to the Hag
our dark truths passed between us like a smouldering joint
shared suffering never articulated leaves a residue
causes an itch that cannot be scratched

I am a curious contradiction like the sun and its shadow

              trying to forget my own fragility
              suspended between two worlds

I exist between night and day   where salt becomes wisdom
and at the end of my bed, a pack of black dogs

on my lips a thickening scar   tastes of toxic soup
a fog and within it a spell cast over the victims
we carry our shame to the dance floor
the crimes of our ancestors   a collective illness
their "original sin" follows us to the after-hours clubs
this time rich boys and bikers   occasionally an allergic reaction
earthbound alchemists we all learned that the rise
      of smoke cannot be hastened
that sometimes *passions are their own punishment*

What Do Frida Kahlo and My Mother Have in Common?

I hope the exit is joyful and I hope never to return.

— FRIDA KAHLO

Where do all the breasts go? Found to be cancerous, excised from women's bodies, for a time they lie on a tin tray. A mound of flesh, a nipple, skin ... my mother's skin   –   pink lying in a lump, in her own blood. Do all the breasts go in one biohazard bag, piled on top of each other? Frightened! They have never been on their own, call out to their sister, but she cannot hear them over all that weeping.

What of legs and arms? Gangrene set in. Blackened. Even so they are missed. Phantom limbs still itch. Hands reach out with nothing left to scratch. The one that remains mourns its companion.

It is not supposed to be like this. We were to go together. All of us at once, not one body part at a time. Yet the remaining bits must carry on, wear bras made for two breasts, pants for two legs, and sweaters for two arms.

Once a part of us has left, it matters not – for our focus is on the living. There will be no one there to grieve as a man in overalls and gloves incinerates our loved ones. No prayers said, flowers offered, ashes scattered. Does this mean that we have *one foot in the grave? One breast in the grave?* For even if no one says it we all know that if not caught soon enough a new word will be introduced.

exile

your mind composes a world it believes true
exiles itself from the heart of the matter
tells and untells truth until it is unrecognizable
on your knees you give up on light,
on truth, on telling and untelling

    it all has nowhere to land

the descent

What would happen if one woman told the truth about her life?
The world would split open.

— MURIEL RUKEYSER

still fifteen she dreamt   her first kiss
black lights   neon clothing
a cobalt-blue bob

         she flew

     a trapeze artist

her journal a record of all that falling

many images expose a digital trail
where high-school students rank her
themselves scrubby boys
not sententious by nature   they egg each other on
claim accidental sightings

she is a collection of disappearances
one who never understood the game
while they opened with a gambit

            a salty sacrifice

she is still the pawn they relish

a song passing many throats
she enters a spiral of silence
inside too many stray sentences
boxes filled with paper dolls
their cut-out shapes swallow her
she falters   cannot unravel it all
a woman with no shadow   she finds a rope

        becomes her own bird of death

the same lines

our bodies house all memories
most lie just below the skin
some go deep into our bones
        marrow houses stories
random, they sort themselves like a deck of cards
occasionally fold in on themselves

they enjoy graveyards   places of worship

        the Chocolate Shop

laugh at tarot readers who skim the surface
offer the same lines
no need to pay someone
     to tell you
        what you already know

nightly visitations

last night I dreamt
your hands on my throat
weight of your body
and all that thrusting
as I was fading ...

later, police in my living room
a distant memory of paper   pens
and note taking   a report never filed
my bent fingers try to hold on to keys
but this one climbs in windows
any crack and he is in again
a sudden burst   my face pushed into the bed
red marks on neck   bent glasses   ripped shirt
and my small son in the bathroom   hiding
this time it is he who tells the police

        this time something is done ...

good medicine

his lips traverse the expanse
of her dancer's back
mouth to skin; he attempts
to remove rote
from all actions

compulsive in his efforts
to save her
his hands find
all manner of unquiet
in her body

in the mirror
his reflection
gazes out
seeks her blessing
divines salvation
in the untying
of her ponytail

outstretched   unfurling
she offers good medicine

he will no longer quibble
about the open umbrella in the hall

she will not mention the dribble
of treacle on the kitchen counter

his shifting suppleness
her shimmering   a sign
there will be no more holding back
they enter knowing wind
would never mar bone

evidence

thigh bone as tuner
vibrates to loss
fingers weep
hold hands of another
but will not touch its own grief
bones in feet carry sadness
burdened they ache
wrinkles on face   evidence
life was hard
smile on mouth a sign

        it is not over

Something and Nothing

Strange the urge to write when one has nothing to say ... but then is anything ever nothing? Creating something out of nothing is something that my mom always said could not be done, yet my dad was always telling her that she was making something out of nothing. If she was right, his nothing was something; something to hide. I will go with her on this matter, there was always something – alcohol, money spent in bars – money meant for milk, rent. What she meant when she said you can't make something out of nothing was, once he spent the money, there would be no milk. The two of them played this something-and-nothing game until she died. Then there was nothing. Home was not home. She was the something that made it a home. He was the nothing that took home away. I tried to tell it differently but I cannot make something out of nothing or is it that "nothing" made something I cannot say?

the temple

my body has things it would like to say

       (others it would like to hide)

it holds my place, keeps my records
remembers all I have said and done

it remembers your touch
is softened by the sound

       of your voice

knows your smell
converses with your body
saying things that neither

of us will ever hear

monkeys in a barrel

arms linked together
we are pulled out
one of us is plastic
orange, lime green
one of us is fake

the *S* of us ...

womblike curves
a place for gestation
invites   undulating
hisses followed by the tracing
of breasts   under fullness
        fingers gently move

towards the heart
      rest there

then full
fingers linger at the top
move down the side, back

tracing *S* again   again
      around breasts

hissing *S* feeling *S*

breasts seek touch   crave mist of hot breath
tongued nipples   ample in the garden
red skinned   a special temptation
that comes with no warning

I dream

in my story streets will travel
noting the migration of birds
their perfect unison   flying as if one
I will walk on the travelling street
its movement will take me to where I need to go
over water   under telephone wires
we will move   as one

pavement   fluid   black   stretching
a flying carpet   many will travel
and some may want to get off
return to the streets of their childhood   where
mothers in kitchens bake cookies and
          fathers in easy chairs
                    smoke pipes   read papers

I will buy a navy peacoat   (the one I never had but wanted)

          but not return to childhood

I dream   of *a room of my own*
     where late nights   lavender   white lace
converse with medicine wheels   ˙

          inhabit the sensuous

          tension   of   between

neat and tidy endings not required

I write undulating hisses
document tracing of breasts
write of skin a little wild
how men know
cross the floor anyway
hold breath
wait   want
circle back
breathe
their desires into her
hand electric
sips from glass deliberate
delicious licking
eyes closed
remembering
how hand on thigh
releases scent   that dangerous place
of letting go

Then

We never knew when he would return or if he would have his car with him. I knew the routine. No car meant tomorrow would be spent looking for it in all the usual spots and us pretending every family does this on Sunday mornings. Sometimes he would bring other people home, the kind of people that knock on bathroom doors while little girls crouch on closed toilet seats afraid to come out, afraid no one else is listening.

I never noticed where he left his keys, his wallet, or his hockey skates. What I would watch for was the tone of his voice, imagined myself a Nancy Drew detecting changes, any slurs, any anger hidden there. Being prepared seemed important – if one can be prepared for knives thrown at kitchen cupboards.

Sometimes he was happy. Whisking Mom off her feet, kissing her forehead on his way to the TV.

& Now

Order is important. At my door
a dish filled with stones for grounding.
One says Goddess in gold letters. A place for keys,
gloves   sunglasses.

Shoes under the bed, in the closet, or by the door
Too many shoes really but then Mom always said
there were two things a girl must have

      a good pair of shoes and a fine coat.

First thing: rings, earrings off.
Then clothes.   That damned underwire
bra exchanged for comfy T-shirt.
      Pants off, tights on
        usually black (they are slimming).

Kettle, tea so nice after a long day   reminds
of evenings on the porch with Mom   everyone
in bed and me feeling so grown-up.

Tonight, my young son asleep
in his room

        safe.

legacy

versions seek wholeness   stories of mothers
in kitchens   wearing aprons   baking squares
        not grandmothers   drinking
bottles of rye   swallowing
pills   after shock
    of electric
administered by doctors in white coats

Fortify

I am removing your throne
                    from my home.

Your reign is over!

You thought I could not see it
hidden   in the corner
        with its view of the TV.
Your hockey chair angled so your eyes
can never meet mine in conversation.

In the other room your privacy
a computer screen   sifting muted women
            who forever submit.

Together you fortify your castle walls.
They are the princesses you can never marry
who will never be the queen you avoid.

dear new-age self

you were always there with a story
a narrative of hope
based on sandy shores
yet many times
our inner instability created wind waves that
blew across our equipoise
creating capillary waves under the skin
but rivulets of hope remained

there was always another temple or ashram
slowed down by shallow water
we crested together   evenly spaced
until the plunging began again
travelling at different speeds
our trajectories unknown
we became that hole in the sea
opposing currents
differing densities
walls of water   we travelled to distant shores
formed deep-water groups
and dreamt of fluid dynamics

high winds
strong currents
within the call and response
of inner oceans
undulating slowly

until sudden movements
generated rogue waves of tutting
disappointment and disillusionment
washed us towards the next guru or teacher
compressed ellipses   eventually disenchanted
we found that turbulent fluctuations could not be avoided
that there is nothing new in this new age

dream kitchen

from my kitchen I see the Fraser River where tugboats
pull covered barges   one hundred times their size
often a single man walks the deck
or leans in the gaping door   smokes
a modern-day Marlon Brando   working on the water
white T-shirt   cigarette pack rolled up in one sleeve

today I watch the water glisten   hear buzz of sawmill
wear apron   chop onions   wipe forehead
          feel tickle in nose
between sniffles   tears   brown rice and lentils simmer
add   mint   a little feta   scoop ingredients into peppers
red   green   yellow   orange   placed on pan
cook at 350 degrees   until flavours   mingle

the cat emerges from his basket   life is simple for him
he sits in the window   watches glisten of water
he too has seen the red tugboat   salient angle of the logs in tow
          knows that some do escape
wend their way downriver   or make their way to shore
I see them on my walks   stray logs in search of a safe harbour
those washed ashore   bask in the sun   as sand   water   abrade
turn them silver grey   smooth their edges

long days in my kitchen   no one knows   I imagine myself
          the tugboat   Brando (some days his lover)
          or best of all the log that got away

I want the water to touch me
          wend me downriver   leave me
                    to float in the moonlight

cowboy songs and carousels ...

some days my inner voice is not peaceful
its mantra more like a crackling radio

on those days it could be a cowboy song
about spilled coffee on kitchen counters
how many times I walk by dirty socks
defenceless   filled with excuses
lying   on the floor
just a few feet away from the laundry basket

but then I pull back the shades
change the station
and the sun streams into the room
Krishna Das in the background   his voice deep
a reminder of all that is good about men

it is then that I laugh at my silly annoyances
how they ride me
                like a carousel horse
pumping up and down to mechanical music

if I close my eyes I can see them
wearing their cowboy hats   floating

                up and
                        down

sometimes on top and other times just below
the surface   going round and round ...

unfinished

at night he calls to me   his grey flesh sinking into his bones
his long   bent fingers point at the dishes in the sink (unwashed)

        the unfinished manuscript

his eyes grow wide when the vacuum comes out
the duster his enemy   smudging   chanting his undoing

     yet he always returns   somehow reborn

his resolve strengthened   finds new ways
creeping under the bed   lying with the dust   a lost sock

     he is patient   waits for that sigh   that look

he is the bogeyman in my closet   the one they said never was

here everything is holy

sweet cedar, take these burdens   heavy they weigh

    my body weakened by the piercing pricks

breaks in skin   not thick   heart full
mind wanting to empty   into a river of tears
my own grief   unholy in my eyes

            unholy in my eyes

sweet cedar, take these burdens   heavy they weigh
so much not mine   yet
others weeping has entered my body

    a hornet's nest under the awning

making a home stingswells   without provocation
my own anger   stifled   unholy in my eyes

      unholy in my eyes

sweet cedar, take these burdens   heavy they weigh
the bows of my shoulders bend   tremble   at your touch
under the tree I stand   your branches   a caress

    here everything is holy

Copper Woman

If I were a colour would I be burnt sienna?
Surely I would be an earth tone.
Matte perhaps. But then there is copper
and I do love a little shine. I could
see myself multicoloured, a weaving,
a Métis sash; with earth tones

        and with the tassels I will keep track of time, mark days.

If I were a vessel, would I be a pitcher? Full   round at the bottom
a wide spout.   White like my dishes or would I be glass?
More delicate   like a vase   narrowing at the top then opening again

to facilitate the outpouring of love   of wine   of water.

I could be cloth, worn loosely around the swaying hips
    of a bare-breasted woman.
Colourful   purple lime green   patterned   but not floral.

Next life I want to be a piece of jewellery worn daily
    by a woman of the woods.
Made of silver   moonstone   obsidian. Mirroring light and dark

    her evenings in the forest.

find

move in closer   you are mine
in the night sky   I call to you
across stretched wires

each day I see you rush
as if you have forgotten   the sacred names
and I can only remember
              for you if you let me

I leave feathers at your door
on the sidewalk by your car
the vehicle of your rushing
it is a good sign that you can still see

my voice the caw   caw   caw of the morning
my wings quietly move
between sound and silence
somewhere in there we are one
find that place   and you will find me

the one who burns skin with his eyes

                              Father will not
                            pass through
                                these lips

his name trapped inside this body
he claimed as his

I seek restitution   the power
      of the Great Mother

her many names pass easily through my lips

sweeten my breath as I offer sweetgrass prayers

her presence infuses every corner of my body

snuffs him out   within this healing smoke

I am at ease with a body that holds the truth

touch

lovers know yielding
how we track inner undulations
in the moonlight
drift in one another's arms
we heave   rush   gush
in ebb and flow of flesh
slaves to our skin

(re)vision

sorting through photos
revisiting memories heavy with guilt
I feel a need to clear old papers
later that night many journals shredded in the co-op office
hours of letting go and I am trembling as my life is cut
into strips of paper   into orderly rows
my own words separated from one another
I am at the threshold of a new life   in need of (re)vision
now there is a sensuous bloom on my lips   tinged red
once full of bitterness but lately they have been sweetened by sacred words
chants and mantras have made my body a home for metaphors
circling the page their call-and-response rhythm informed
by the tabla player   a red-headed boy   so young to be a seeker
and I wonder what took me so long

apocalyptic Sunday

i
she never knew where food came from
in grocery aisles   bananas from far-off lands   abundant ripe
olives from Italy   jetted across a sky now bare
but now she must learn about the earth's rhythms

   what can she plant here

the three sisters   are making a comeback

   beans climbing   corn   squash

companion planting   she is creating a microclimate

   the soil   dry   her *kokum*

all the ancestors under her feet   whisper

   offer themselves

ii

until today she had never buried a body
she had never stood over a grave that she had dug
shovel in hand   sweat on brow merges with tears
once the grave is ready   how to prepare the body
there is little water   too few blankets yet she feels the need
to wash his face   his hands   to wrap him
in their favourite blanket
      the one they shared under the stars
as they listened to trees singing for water

iii

she never thought she would miss the sounds of traffic
the steady flow   tires on wet pavement
there are no cellphones ringing   no crowded coffee shops

     where music is played too loud

and no one speaks of the stars singing

this quiet stretches across the country   death swallows all sounds
    too few birds chirp   no bees buzz
somewhere water is still falling   polluted it crawls towards oceans
where plastic lingers   pristine water   a memory
the trees call out to her   but she has nothing to give them

mother

how you echo through my life
each day that you are gone the sound of your voice fades a little more
the feel of your cheek on my cheek   so long ago
yet lately time is on speed   hurling me towards you
but I put the brakes on   take multivitamins
daily walks to ward off our heavenly reunion
I don't want my son to be motherless
without you I wandered in and out   weaving a life
but like my knitting there were holes I could not fix
so each night I unravelled it all   tried to start over
without you   there are holes
I cannot fix   without you I am a motherless adult
child of Lorraine Emily Denham   granddaughter of Jónína Buason
your mother and I share a name   but she had 17 children
I had one but wanted two   remember, Momma, how you came to me
in my dreams   how you sat on the chair by my bed to comfort me
when I lost my girl   a daughterless mother   a motherless daughter
I have no reflection   yet there are echoes of you everywhere
in picture frames you smile   still   inside I long to see you
I walk a tightrope between you   and the fate that awaits me
I walk a tightrope between you and my son
between you and my disappearing daughter
and then my son smiles   holds up his tomato plant and I see you
shining in his eyes   you offer so many clues
that you are not gone   you still echo throughout my life

on Indian time

inner metronome   too often silenced

   – moving too slowly for the world –

tick of clock   pulls us towards some future we did not dream

too many have forgotten

dreaming ourselves a new future takes time

      not tick of clock time

but footsteps bare   touch the earth time

leave the tobacco   call the ancestors time

honour our bones   feel the land time

    thank you for making me human time

Mystery Man

i

My father tells my son war stories   shows him medals I never knew he had.
In boxes they find a newspaper article about a "mystery man"   who in
The Pas scored a perfect game bowling.   The "mystery man" not
wanting attention snuck out the back door.

The article mentions at the end that the mystery man was the younger
brother of my aunt Val.

ii

The summer of 2009 my father took me to the old churchyard   told me
of our family's connection to Louis Riel.   The man who has never said
he is an "Indian" showed me gravestones of Métis ancestors from the
Red River settlement, ancestors who knew Louis well. He does not
know what became of the letters Louis sent.

Next day he was silent again.

iii

On my next visit to Winnipeg, I tell my family that we got a great deal
on a luxury suite at the Place Louis Riel. We are thrilled with our room.
I mention that sometimes bookings from Expedia do not live up to the
pictures, but this one certainly did. My brother looks worried.

It has a bad reputation, you know.

My friend and I laugh, tell them how on our arrival we were concerned
to discover that the door between the parking lot and the elevator was
fortified like a skid-row pawnshop, and that we had to be buzzed in.
My friend also recounts that on our first ride up to our room the elevator
doors opened, and inside there were four *drunk Indians*, all big men, and
that for a moment we hesitated ... but then the familiar laugh, the nod,
the one that says, *You're one of us*. It told us that we were okay. But when
I glance at my father I can see that *drunk Indians* has fallen on him like
meteor debris. This, the man who never admits to being "Indian," can
still be hurt by those two words flung so casually by those who do not
know his pain.

iv

The following summer, my father tells my son that he was once offered a $5,000-a-year contract with the Montreal Canadiens farm team and a tryout with the NHL club. But he declined. Instead he kept his appointment for testing as an air traffic controller. He had a family to feed. Hearing this, my baby brother laughs and says, *It only took us forty years to get this story out of him.*

My father has always told my son the important stories. Man to man since he was five, my son is the one he wants to talk to.

Manitou Lake

together we float   praying
for another life   another body
                one that does not ache

this land reverberates   its skin stretched tightly
drumbeats echo   when quiet you can hear
        the sounds of the buffalo
and a time when the land still spoke

heavy with salt, a medicine wheel waits
on the other side   exiled

written words have no place here
only prayers   raised hands

this land respects no map
its shifting its own

the water calls, *Manitou   Manitou*

pulls me closer
to some memory of before
of bones   of ancestors

        and behind my eyes I feel

knotted hands hold sticks not stones
        burnt sienna skin
its undoing lost in the wind   it sings

        Hiya   *Hiya*   *Hiya*

there is no sinking here   only
copper   water   once sacred

now the sky outside cannot touch our skin
        what little I know   of home   of water
I am here, but part of me is always there   bone to bone
my marrow still sings your songs
recalls your name *Manitou   Manitou*

Dear Gabriel,

By now you know they have hanged me. I am here with God now and
heard you were working in the Buffalo Bill show. Things didn't exactly
work out for either of us. Sure wish that you had not listened to me.
There I was pacing back and forth with that darned cross in my hands,
praying for victory. I should have known that this "White" God was not
on our side. I can tell you that He is not who He says he is. He says I got in
here by the skin of my teeth. Apparently, God did not care much for those
who excommunicated me, and the prayers of Father André really helped.
That and the fact that I made my last confession before they hanged me.
Turns out that confession really works, so no hell for me. That is, unless
you call this White God's "heaven" hell. Pray for me, my friend.

But this is not why I write you. I want to say I am sorry that you listened
to me. You knew we were in harm's way and that peace was not an
option. I so regret not allowing you to lead the fight your way. Night
harassments were not enough. Our reward for holding back was not
brought forth by my prayers. My God abandoned us. I know you tried
to argue with me but that in the end you acquiesced because you
thought I was a prophet. For a time I thought I was a prophet too, but
we both know that in this case I was wrong. I see now that Middleton
was afraid, that they had many wounded from our first encounter.
While we held back, they frantically set up a field ambulance. I kept
insisting that some miracle would come and bring us to victory.

I see now that my fanatical insistence that the English would come to
understand our cause was wrong. They had the Canadian media
reporting on us. Many knew our circumstances, and it was only our
Québécois brothers who sided openly with us. Apparently, the story of

our struggles went around the world. We got quite famous, aye ...
probably why you got the job with the Wild West show. That and the
fact that you clean up nice. That buckskin coat and your sharpshooting
let them all know that we were not so easy to defeat. I hear some think
I was a madman and others a prophet. I am not sure now if I was either.
All I know is that I am forever grateful for your friendship and I wish
I had stayed closer to the redskin ways like you did. I am pretty sure that
it was university and the Church that left me in the so-called logical side
of my brain ... I see now it was the "White" side of my brain that left
me hoping and praying for a peaceful outcome. I did not know that
the Orangemen government would never respect us since we were
half-breeds and in their eyes not deserving of negotiations. Probably
did not help that so many of us were Catholics.

Also because I am here now with God, I am no longer sure that we
needed a new Church. The red in me knows that our land is our Church
and had I not committed myself to this White God I might still be
wandering the land of my people. An ancestor who they could call on.
I pray that you become this one day, that they at least will have you to
turn to.

    Regards,
    Louis

PS
I was right about a few things. One day I will be declared a hero, not a
traitor. Apparently, our people will sleep a little longer than one hundred
years, but it will be the artists who will give them back their spirits.

Otipemisiwak (the people who own themselves)

bones the receptacle of all that we have seen and done
    all that our ancestors have seen and done
their story   our story
    sagas travel the centuries

in Lake of the Woods you feel home
have no idea why   until years later you read
the Assiniboine inhabited that part of the world
your body knew   long before you knew

    you were a descendant

Assiniboine   a stone Sioux

    still nomadic you wander

when quiet memories bleed through
with Christ on a hill   you know how he feels
the Bible unrecognizable in his presence
you a simple Essene woman sit quietly

      there is nothing to say

moving through time
a table   many men   ready to fight
smell of deerskin coats   gunpowder in your nose
their powder flasks   bullets quickly filled
with sulphur   charcoal   saltpetre

you a rebel stand in a river of time, and when the healer asks

what your lesson was in this life

   no thought

your lips form words

       I want to own myself

Notes on the Poems

epigraph

These are the inspiring words of Jeannette Armstrong, quoted in
Joy Harjo and Gloria Birds, eds., *Reinventing the Enemy's Language:
Contemporary Native Women's Writings of North America* (New York:
W.W. Norton, 1997), 498–99.

the doorbell

I thank Kathleen Harrison for the phrase "dark potential." I met
Kathleen when I had the good fortunate to moderate a panel discussion
titled *Heart of the Earth: The Renaissance of Feminine Medicine in the
Conduct of Human Affairs* at the 2011 Spirit Medicine Conference in
Vancouver. Kathleen and fellow panel member Chenoa Egawa both
brought much wisdom to the conference. When Kathleen mentioned
that many tribal cultures valued those who could see a "dark potential,"
I felt vindicated, because this unique ability is not always valued in
contemporary culture – in fact, it is often regarded with suspicion.
This gift comes with great responsibility; when and how to share these
visions was something I had to learn.

collective history

"passions are their own punishment" is a phrase Kat Duff uses in
The Alchemy of Illness (New York: Pantheon, 1993).

the same lines

The Chocolate Shop was a popular Winnipeg restaurant on Portage
Avenue near Main Street. Long before the new-age movement and the
popularity of psychics, locals and visitors frequented the place, not only
for the food, but also for psychic readings. On his blog, Trevor Thorkelson,
a well-known Winnipeg-based psychic, recalls that in Winnipeg there
was "a very different attitude about intuitive / psychic reading [due to]
the rich multicultural background of this city. Where people come
together but honor their roots, as well as the rich sense of folklore that

many of us are proud of." At the Chocolate Shop, where Thorkelson often worked, you ordered a reading along with your food and a psychic would come to your table.

on Indian time
This poem was inspired by the storyteller Woody Morrison's Haida teachings on time.

Manitou Lake
Manitou Lake, in western Saskatchewan, has a mineral content like no other body of water on Turtle Island. Sometimes compared to the Dead Sea, its salinity is five times higher than that of ocean water. You cannot sink in it. My husband first introduced me to the healing properties of Manitou Lake. Although I was not relieved of fibromyalgia pain, as I had hoped, after just one afternoon in the water, a large third-degree burn scar I had for years disappeared. I've wondered ever since what other miracles could happen if I spent a week or more there.

Cree legend tells how three braves first discovered the healing power of the waters when, too sick with smallpox to travel, their fellow warriors left them behind near the lake. One of the men, hoping to cool his fever, bathed in the lake and drank the water before passing out, only to wake up with no fever or lesions. When he realized that the water had cured him, he brought the other two men down to the water and they too were cured.

Once a popular tourist destination on the Canadian Pacific Railway line, Manitou Lake and the spa there fell into disrepair in the mid-1950s. When my husband and I visited in 2011, we felt deep sadness at the condition of this once-sacred site. This poem is an attempt to reconcile the history of that land and the many losses experienced by the First Nations and Métis people of the area.

Dear Gabriel
This poem was inspired by Joseph Boyden's book *Louis Riel and Gabriel Dumont* (Toronto: Penguin, 2010).

Otipemisiwak

Otipemisiwak is a Cree word that has been used to describe the Métis people. I'm grateful to Lii Michif Family and Community Services, who published the following summary of the word on their website:

"The Métis were – and are – a people distinguished by their independence, individuality and resilience. The Cree referred to Métis people as *Otipemisiwak*, which, loosely translated, means 'the people who own themselves' or 'the people who govern themselves.' Métis people have a history of independence, self-governance and democratically elected leadership that endures to the present day. They have consistently and continuously sought the recognition and protection of inherent rights in all aspects of their lives."

Acknowledgements

I have many people to thank for their close editorial attention to this book. First, a special thanks to Betsy Warland and her Vancouver Manuscript Intensive. Betsy's gentle guidance assisted me in finding my way with this book. Without her, it would not have happened. Also, many thanks to Garry Thomas Morse, Greg Gibson, and Ann-Marie Metten of Talonbooks for their patient and detailed efforts with the substantive and copy edits. All of these changes, as subtle as many of them were, brought cohesiveness to the book.

And for their suggestions, encouragement, and inspiration, I offer my thanks to Ingrid Rose and her *writing from the body* classes, where many of the pieces originated, to our beloved Continuum teacher, Doris Maranda, to Oriah Mountain Dreamer, Joanne Arnott, and the Aboriginal Writers Collective – West Coast. I also give thanks to Miranda Pearson (my first poetry mentor), to those I have sat with in writing circles, and to Simon Fraser University's Writer's Studio, where I discovered I was a poet. Lastly, I am so grateful to my foundation, my dear husband, Garry Ward, who has been my biggest supporter/editor/mentor. Thank you for your continued love and patience.

And thanks to my somewhat dysfunctional family for all the rich material. I love you all. I hope that you will still be speaking to me after reading what are my own memories of our life together, flawed as they may be. I hope that each of you will keep in mind that in some cases liberal poetic licence has been used to fill in the blanks, which were numerous.

Many thanks to Les Smith for the cover design and to Ayelet Tsabari for the author photo, to the staff at Talonbooks, and to the Canada Council for the Arts for a writing grant that got this book started.

Earlier versions of some of these poems were first published in various journals and anthologies including: *ricepaper*'s Aboriginal & Asian Canadian Writers issue; *V6A: Writing from the Vancouver's Downtown Eastside* (Arsenal Pulp, 2012); *between earth and sky* (Silver Bow, 2012); *Royal City Poets Anthology* (Silver Bow, 2013); *home & away* (a chapbook anthology); and *Wordplay*, the newsletter of the Royal City Literary Arts Society.

"dream kitchen" won first prize in the Royal City Literary Arts Write On! Contest.

Photo: Ayelet Tsabari

Jónína Kirton is a Métis/Icelandic poet and author who lives and works in Vancouver. She graduated from Simon Fraser University's Writer's Studio in 2007 and attended the Emerging Aboriginal Writer's Residency at the Banff Centre in 2008. Actively involved with the Aboriginal Writers Collective – West Coast, she coordinated the first National Indigenous Writers Conference in Vancouver 2013.

Kirton's work has been featured in numerous anthologies and literary journals, including *Ricepaper*'s Asian & Aboriginal issue, *V6A: Writing from Vancouver's Downtown Eastside, Other Tongues: Mixed Race Women Speak Out, Pagan Edge, First Nations Drum, Toronto Quarterly*, and *Quills Canadian Poetry Magazine*. She won first prize and two honourable mentions in the 2013 Royal City Literary Arts Society's Write On! Contest and was a finalist in the 2013 Burnaby Writers' Society Writing Contest. Awarded a Canada Council grant in 2009 to complete *page as bone – ink as blood*, she is currently researching her next book.